KIM THOMPSON

TABLE OF CONTENTS

A Pelican Book

Teaching Tips for Caregivers and Teachers:

Research shows that one of the best ways for students to learn a new topic is to read about it.

Before Reading

- Read the title and predict what the book will be about.
- Read the "Words to Know" and discuss the meaning of each word.
- Read the back cover to see what the book is about.

During Reading

- When a student gets to a word that is unknown, ask them to look at the rest of the sentence to find clues to help with the meaning of the unknown word.
- Motivate students with praise and encouragement.

After Reading

- Discuss the main idea of the book.
- Ask students to give one detail that they learned in the book.

SIGHT WORDS

can
has
in
kinds
of
put
see
these
this
you

Words to Know

dimes

nickels

groups

pennies

money

quarters

You can see kinds of **money**.

You can put money in **groups**.

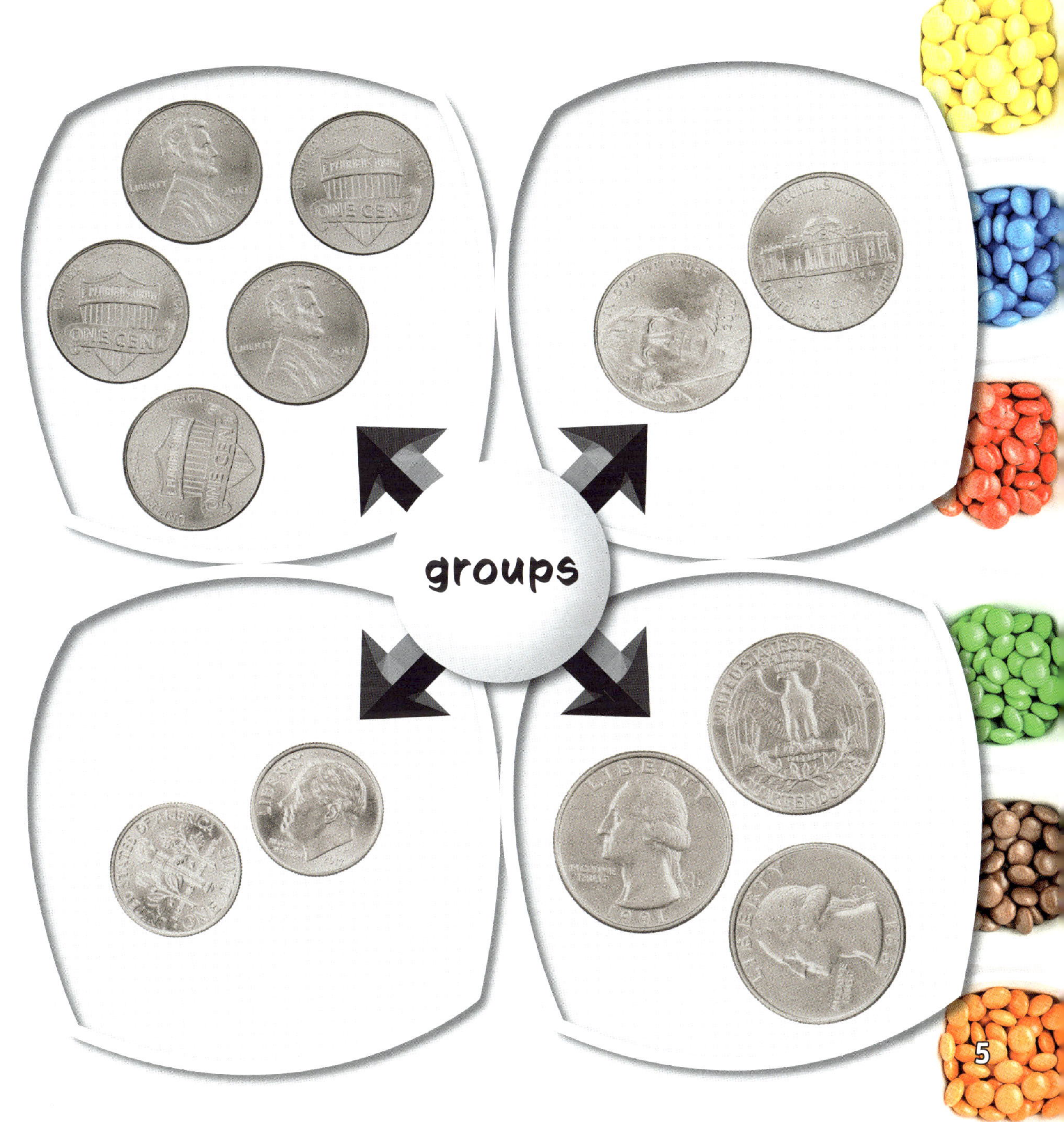
groups

This group has **pennies.**

1¢

This group has **nickels**.

5¢

This group has **dimes**.

10¢

This group has **quarters.**

25¢

Can you group these?

Count the money on page 15.
Which group has 5¢?
Which group has 10¢?
Which group has 20¢?

ONE CENT
LIBERTY
IN GOD WE TRUST
E PLURIBUS UNUM
UNITED STATES OF AMERICA
MONTICELLO
FIVE CENTS
QUARTER DOLLAR

Index

Written by: Kim Thompson
Design by: Jen Bowers
Series Development: James Earley

Photos: cover: border top ©2019 Cristina Ionescu/Shutterstock, border bottom ©2018 3d_kot/Shutterstock, images: ©2021 Somchai Som/Shutterstock; p.3 and 4 ©2010 dvande/ Shutterstock; p.5, 6, 8, 10, 12, 14 and 15 ©2019 DnDavis/ Shutterstock; p.7 ©2009 Craig Wactor/Shutterstock, p.7, 9, 11, and 13 ©2013 anntavi/Shutterstock

Library of Congress PCN Data
Money /Kim Thompson
Let's Sort
ISBN 978-1-6389-7952-4 (hard cover)
ISBN 979-8-8873-5011-0 (paperback)
ISBN 979-8-8873-5070-7 (EPUB)
ISBN 979-8-8873-5129-2 (eBook)
Library of Congress Control Number: 2022942696

Printed in the United States of America.

Seahorse Publishing Company
www.seahorsepub.com

Published in the United States
Seahorse Publishing
PO Box 771325
Coral Springs, FL 33077